STEM Projects in **MINECRAFT®**

The Unofficial Guide to

Making Art in MINECRAFT®

SAM KEPPELER

PowerKiDS press
New York

Published in 2020 by The Rosen Publishing Group, Inc.
29 East 21st Street, New York, NY 10010

First Edition

Editor: Greg Roza
Book Design: Rachel Rising
Illustrator: Matias Lapegüe

Photo Credits: Cover, 1,3,5,6,8,10,12,14,16,18,20,22,23,24 (background) Evgeniy Dzyuba/Shutterstock.com; p.4 Poznyakov/Shutterstock.com; p.5 Anadolu Agency/Anadolu Agency/Getty Images; p. 6, 8, 12,14,16,18, 20 (insert) Levent Konuk/Shutterstock.com; p. 9 dobrik/Shutterstock.com; p. 11 Zhao jian kang/Shutterstock.com; p. 15 Aleksandar Todorovic/Shutterstock.com; p. 16 railway fx/Shutterstock.com; p. 19 LeManna/Shutterstock.com; p. 21 SpeedKingz/Shutterstock.com; p. 22 se media/Shutterstock.com.

Cataloging-in-Publication Data

Names: Keppeler, Sam.
Title: The unofficial guide to making art in Minecraft ® / Sam Keppeler.
Description: New York : PowerKids Press, 2020. | Series: STEM projects in Minecraft | Includes glossary and index.
Identifiers: ISBN 9781725310544 (pbk.) | ISBN 9781725310568 (library bound) | ISBN 9781725310551 (6 pack)
Subjects: LCSH: Art–Technique–Juvenile literature. | Minecraft (Game) – Juvenile literature.
Classification: LCC GV1469.M55 K47 2020 | DDC 794.8–dc23

Manufactured in the United States of America

CPSIA Compliance Information: Batch #CWPK20. For Further Information contact Rosen Publishing, New York, New York at 1-800-237-9932.

Contents

For Art's Sake

What is art? It's more than drawing a picture or making something with clay—although it includes those things too. People think of art in many different ways. One meaning of the word is using imagination, skill, and creativity to make something, often something that looks nice, tells a story, or brings out emotions in those who see it.

Humans have been making art for many thousands of years—nearly as long as there have been humans on Earth. We use many different tools to create art. You can make art in *Minecraft*, too. All you need is your imagination!

These pictures of human hands, found in a cave in Borneo, may be the oldest rock art on Earth.

So Many Kinds

Paintings and drawings can be art. So can sculptures, **photographs**, certain **textiles**, and many different crafts. Music, dance, and writing can be art, too! Architecture, or planning and creating buildings, is an art form.

You'll need supplies to create art in *Minecraft*, just like in real life. How you get them will depend on what **mode** you play in. In Creative mode, you'll have all the **materials** you need to make things—including art! You can fly, too, which makes many things easier. In Survival mode, you have to find and collect everything you need, both to live and to make art.

MINECRAFT MANIA

You can be a photographer in *Minecraft*, in a way. Most ways of playing the game, including computers and gaming systems, have a way to take a screenshot, or a picture of what you're seeing on the screen.

See a beautiful *Minecraft* sunset or a really cool scene that you want to remember? Take a screenshot and use it for your computer wallpaper!

A Splash of Color

Visual art doesn't have to be colorful, but it can be! There are ways to add color to many *Minecraft* materials. Like the first dyes humans used thousands of years ago, these dyes come from things in nature, especially plants. You can use flowers, beets, cacti, and cocoa beans (and a few other things) to make *Minecraft* dyes.

Once you have your dyes, there are many things you can color. You can dye wool (and sheep!), terra-cotta, glass, armor, firework stars, banner patterns, concrete powder, beds, and more. You can combine colors to make other colors.

MINECRAFT MANIA

There are 16 dye colors in *Minecraft*. They are: red, orange, yellow, lime, green, cyan (blue green), light blue, blue, purple, magenta (a purplish-red color), pink, white, light gray, gray, black, and brown.

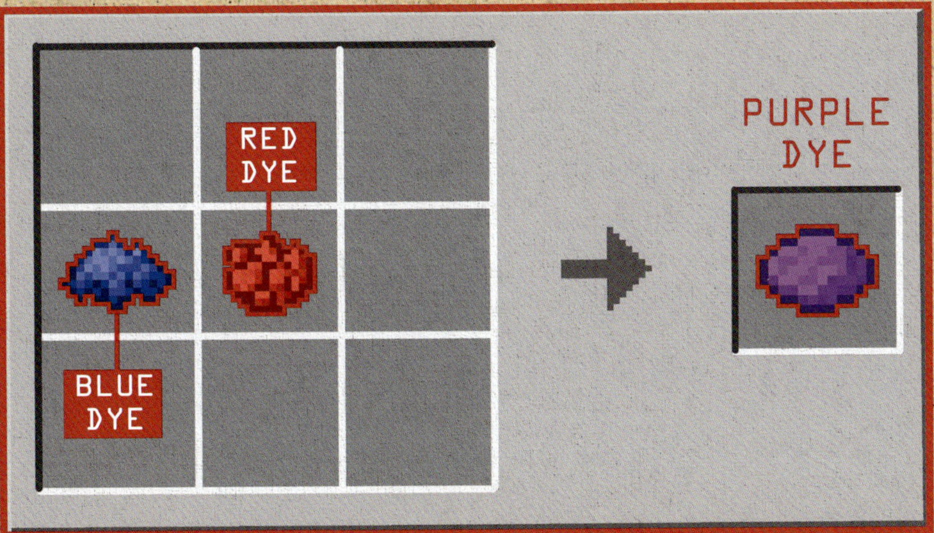

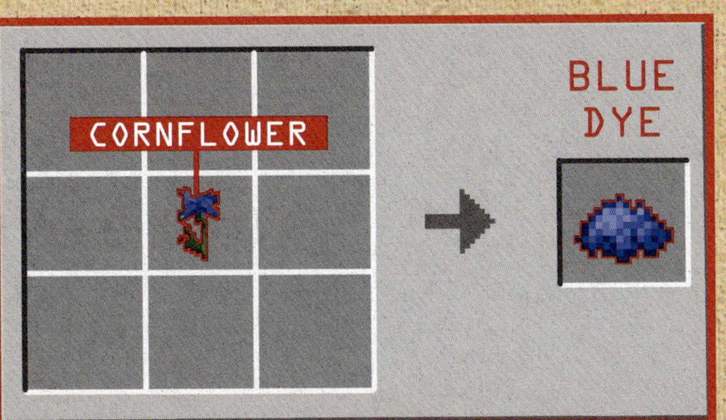

Once, only kings could wear a special shade of purple called Tyrian purple. This is because the dye had to be made from a tiny part of a tiny sea snail that only lived in one place! It was very expensive. In *Minecraft*, you can make purple by combining blue and red dyes.

sea snail shell

Terra-Cotta

In the real world, the word "terra-cotta" refers to something made of clay that's been fired, or had heat applied to harden it. Terra-cotta items are naturally reddish brown. They can be plain and useful or very beautiful. Artists in ancient China and other places made statues of the material. People also use it in architecture.

You can't make statues of terra-cotta in *Minecraft*—not unless you make those statues out of blocks of the material! But you can use terra-cotta for decoration and building. You can dye it different colors, too. However, first you need to collect a lot of clay.

Thousands of terra-cotta soldiers surround the burial site of China's first emperor, Qin Shi Huang Di. He died in 210 BC.

There are two ways to get terra-cotta in *Minecraft's* Survival mode. You can find blocks of plain or colored terra-cotta naturally in mesa (or badlands) **biomes**. You can also find blocks of raw clay, which is light gray, underwater. When you break a block (it's fastest with a shovel), you'll get four balls of clay.

You can **smelt** the balls of clay in a furnace to make bricks and combine four bricks into a brick block. Or, you can combine the balls of clay to make a block of clay again and smelt that. When you do it this way, you make terra-cotta!

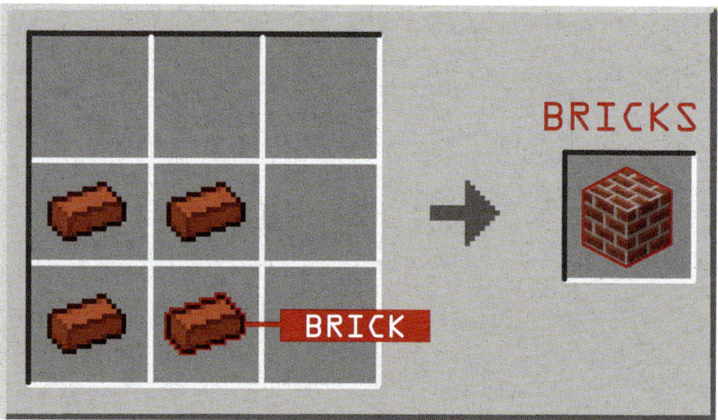

MINECRAFT MANIA

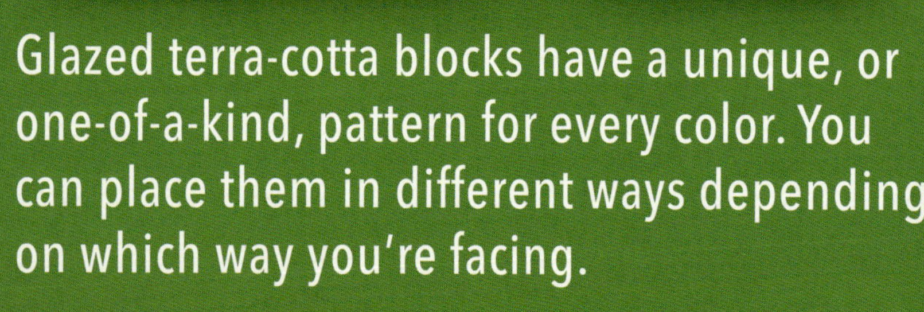

Glazed terra-cotta blocks have a unique, or one-of-a-kind, pattern for every color. You can place them in different ways depending on which way you're facing.

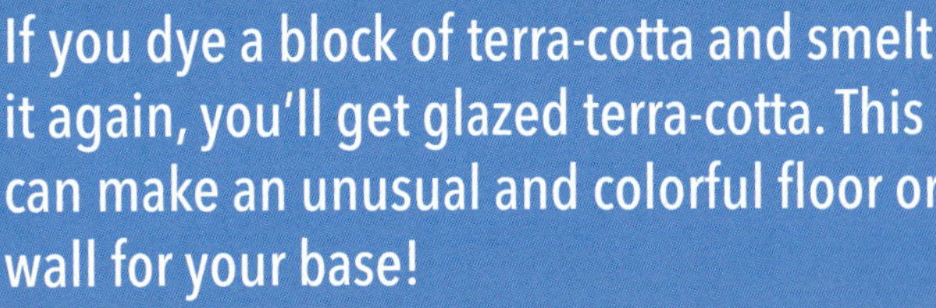
If you dye a block of terra-cotta and smelt it again, you'll get glazed terra-cotta. This can make an unusual and colorful floor or wall for your base!

Wild and Woolly

Did you know that cloth can be art? People have been making beautiful **fabrics** with materials such as wool, cotton, and silk for thousands of years. They dye yarn and other fibers and weave them or print them with different patterns.

Wool can't do quite as much in *Minecraft*, but you can dye it. Then you can turn the dyed wool into items such as beds, banners, and carpets. With a block of wool and eight sticks, you can make a painting. When you put it on a wall, you'll get one of 26 pictures, but you can't pick what you'll get.

MINECRAFT MANIA

You get wool in *Minecraft* by **shearing** or killing sheep. It's better to shear them, because then they'll regrow their wool and you can shear them again.

This woman in Guatemala is making brightly colored handmade textiles. Textiles can be plain or they can be art forms like this.

Heraldry

Heraldry is an art that deals with family **symbols**. These symbols started out on flags and shields in **medieval** Europe. Using dyes, you can create your own symbols on banners (and, in some types of *Minecraft*, shields) in the game. In fact, *Minecraft* uses many of the same words for certain patterns.

In both heraldry and *Minecraft*, "chief" means the top of a banner and "base" means the bottom. "Sinister" means left and "dexter" means right. A "pale" is an up-and-down stripe. A "fess" is a center side-to-side stripe. You can combine these and many other patterns to make many **designs**.

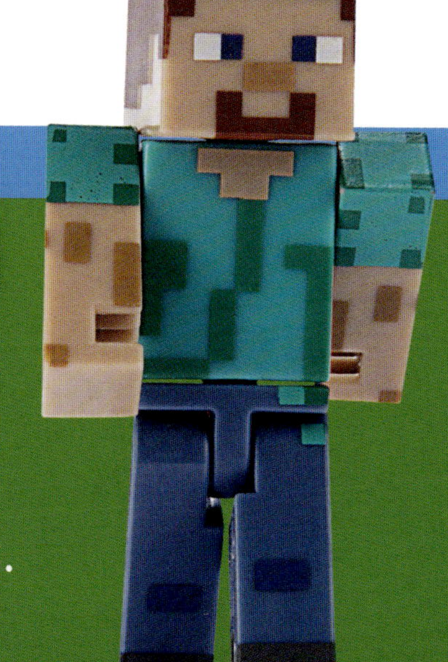

MINECRAFT MANIA

You can use up to six designs on each *Minecraft* banner. That means you can make thousands of combinations! You can also add shapes with a daisy or other items.

An "X" shape on a banner is called a "saltire" in both *Minecraft* and real-world heraldry. The flag of Scotland, shown on p. 16, has a white saltire on a blue background. The steps here show how to make a Scottish flag in *Minecraft*.

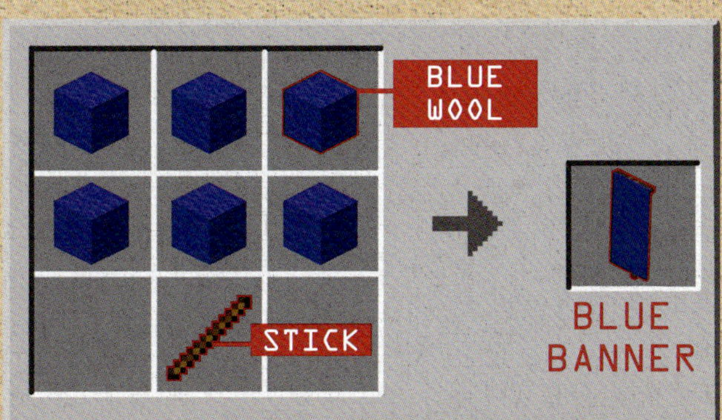

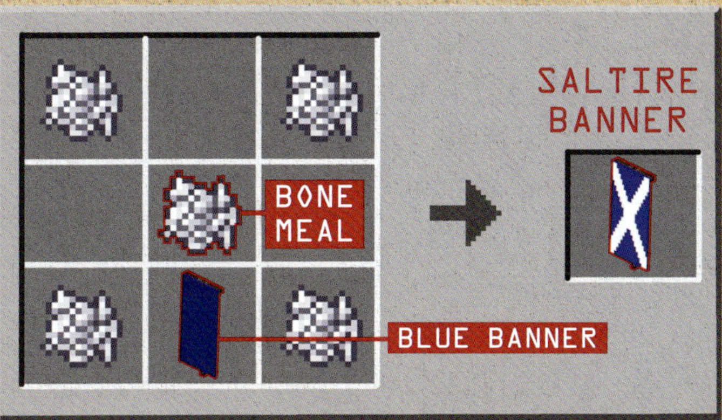

Map Art

Map art is another way to make paintings for the walls of your *Minecraft* buildings. First, you need to craft a blank map using nine pieces of paper. Then, you need to take the map to a flat, open area and activate it. Move to the center of the map so the map will show anything you build on it.

Next, use different colored blocks to create a picture in the open area. Whatever you create will appear on the map! Making map art can take some time, but there's no end to the paintings you can create. Have fun experimenting!

MINECRAFT MANIA

You can make an item frame for your map art with one piece of leather and eight sticks. You don't need to put a map in one, though. You can use a clock, a sword, or a flower–any *Minecraft* item you want hanging on your wall!

This creeper face pattern on a map is an easy one to create with green and black wool blocks. What else could you create?

Music and Words

Music and writing are art, too! You can create both in *Minecraft*. To make a book other players can read, you first have to create a book with one piece of leather and three pieces of paper. Then, combine it with an ink sac (from a *Minecraft* squid) and a feather (from a *Minecraft* chicken). This is called a book and **quill**.

A *Minecraft* note block is made of eight blocks of wood and one piece of redstone dust. It plays a musical note when a player hits it or it's powered by redstone. You can change a note block's tone by clicking on it.

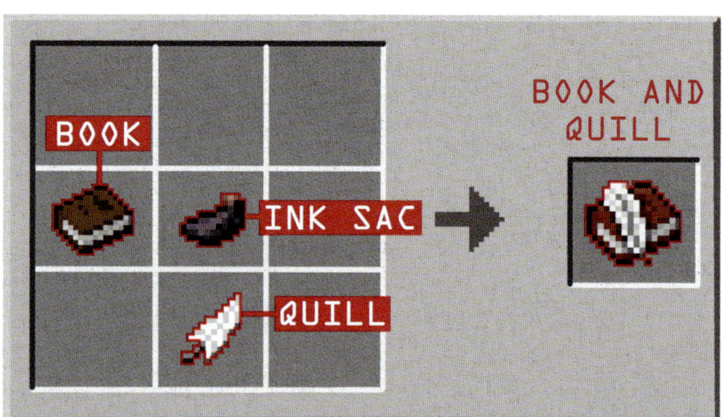

MINECRAFT MANIA

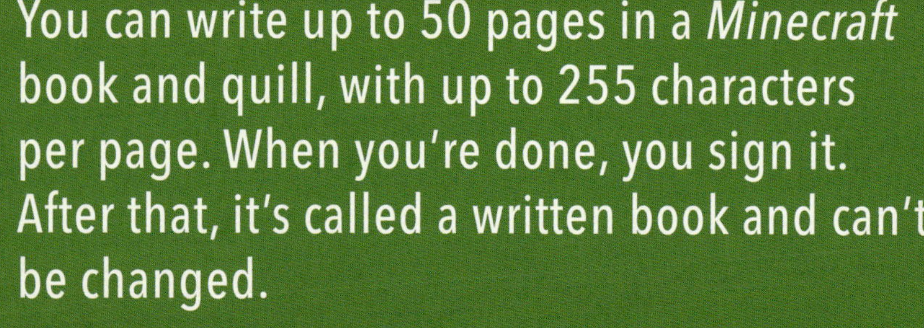

You can write up to 50 pages in a *Minecraft* book and quill, with up to 255 characters per page. When you're done, you sign it. After that, it's called a written book and can't be changed.

Depending on what material is under a note block, it will sound like a different instrument. For example, a note block with a block of stone under it will sound like a bass drum.

Making Mods

You can make your *Minecraft* creations even more exciting with modifications, or mods. Using a computer program called ScriptCraft, you can create new blocks, change the way the game functions, and make your own games. Imagine what you could create! Perhaps you could add animal heraldry designs to banners. You could create new dye colors such as dark blue, pale orange, or violet.

If you're interested in learning how to create mods in *Minecraft*, visit the website below. You'll find the information needed to get started with ScriptCraft and build your own *Minecraft* mods.

https://scriptcraftjs.org/

Glossary

biome: A natural community of plants and animals, such as a forest or desert.

design: To create the pattern or shape of something. Also, the pattern or shape of something.

fabric: Woven or knitted material.

material: Something from which something else can be made.

medieval: Having to do with the Middle Ages, a time in European history from about 500 to 1500.

mode: A form of something that is different from other forms of the same thing.

photograph: A picture made by a camera.

quill: The hollow main part of a feather, a big, stiff feather, or a pen made from such a feather.

shear: To cut the wool off an animal.

smelt: To heat to separate metals.

symbol: Something that stands for something else.

textile: A kind of cloth that is woven or knit.

Index

Websites

Due to the changing nature of Internet links, PowerKids Press has developed an online list of websites related to the subject of this book. This site is updated regularly. Please use this link to access the list:
www.powerkidslinks.com/stemmc/art